# DANGER IN THE DEEP:

## Surviving Shark Attacks

# DANGER IN THE DEEP:

## Surviving Shark Attacks

Joyce Zoldak

 Mason Crest Publishers

**DANGER IN THE DEEP:** Surviving Shark Attacks

MASON CREST PUBLISHERS INC.
370 Reed Road
Broomall, Pennsylvania 19008
(866)MCP-BOOK (toll free)
www.masoncrest.com

Because the stories in this series are told by real people, in some cases names have been changed to protect the privacy of the individuals.

First Printing
9 8 7 6 5 4 3 2 1
 ISBN 978-1-4222-0449-8 (series)
 ISBN 978-1-4222-1462-6 (series) (pbk.)

    Library of Congress Cataloging-in-Publication Data

Zoldak, Joyce.
 Danger in the deep : surviving shark attacks / Joyce Zoldak.
    p. cm. — (Survivors, ordinary people, extraordinary circumstances)
 Includes bibliographical references and index.
 ISBN 978-1-4222-0511-2 (alk. paper)
 ISBN 978-1-4222-1475-6 (pbk.)
 1. Shark attacks—United States—Juvenile literature.
 2. Shark attacks—Prevention—United States—Juvenile literature.  I. Title.
 QL638.93.Z65 2009
 597.3092'2—dc22
                                    2008023317

Design by MK Bassett-Harvey.
Produced by Harding House Publishing Service, Inc.
www.hardinghousepages.com
Cover design by Andrew Mezvinsky.
Printed in The Hashemite Kingdom of Jordan.

# CONTENTS

# Introduction

Each of us is confronted with challenges and hardships in our daily lives. Some of us, however, have faced extraordinary challenges and severe adversity. Those who have lived—and often thrived—through affliction, illness, pain, tragedy, cruelty, fear, and even near-death experiences are known as survivors. We have much to learn from survivors and much to admire.

Survivors fascinate us. Notice how many books, movies, and television shows focus on individuals facing—and overcoming—extreme situations. *Robinson Crusoe* is probably the earliest example of this, followed by books like the *Swiss Family Robinson*. Even the old comedy *Gilligan's Island* appealed to this fascination, and today we have everything from the Tom Hanks' movie *Castaway* to the hit reality show *Survivor* and the popular TV show *Lost*.

What is it about survivors that appeals so much to us? Perhaps it's the message of hope they give us. These people have endured extreme challenges—and they've overcome them. They're ordinary people who faced extraordinary situations. And if they can do it, just maybe we can too.

This message is an appropriate one for young adults. After all, adolescence is a time of daily challenges. Change is everywhere in their lives, demanding that they adapt and cope with a constantly shifting reality. Their bodies change in response to increasing levels of sex hormones; their thinking processes change as their brains develop, allowing them to think in more abstract ways; their social lives change as new people and peers become more important. Suddenly, they experience the burning need to form their own identities. At the same time, their emotions are labile and unpredictable. The people they were as children may seem to have disappeared beneath the onslaught of new emotions, thoughts, and sensations. Young adults have to deal with every single one of these changes, all at the same time. Like many of the survivors whose stories are told in this series, adolescents' reality is often a frightening, confusing, and unfamiliar place.

Young adults are in crises that are no less real simply because these are crises we all live through (and most of us survive!) Like all survivors, young adults emerge from their crises transformed; they are not the people they were before. Many of them bear scars they will carry with them for life—and yet these scars can be integrated into their new identities. Scars may even become sources of strength.

In this book series, young adults will have opportunities to learn from individuals faced with tremendous struggles. Each individual has her own story, her own set of circumstances and challenges, and her own way of coping and surviving. Whether facing cancer or abuse, terrorism or natural disaster, genocide or school violence, all the survivors who tell their stories in this series have found the ability and will to carry on despite the trauma. They cope, persevere, persist, and live on as a person changed forever by the ordeal and suffering they endured. They offer hope and wisdom to young adults: if these people can do it, so can they!

These books offer a broad perspective on life and its challenges. They will allow young readers to become more self-aware of the demanding and difficult situations in their own lives—while at the same time becoming more compassionate toward those who have gone through the unthinkable traumas that occur in our world.

— Andrew M. Kleiman, M.D.

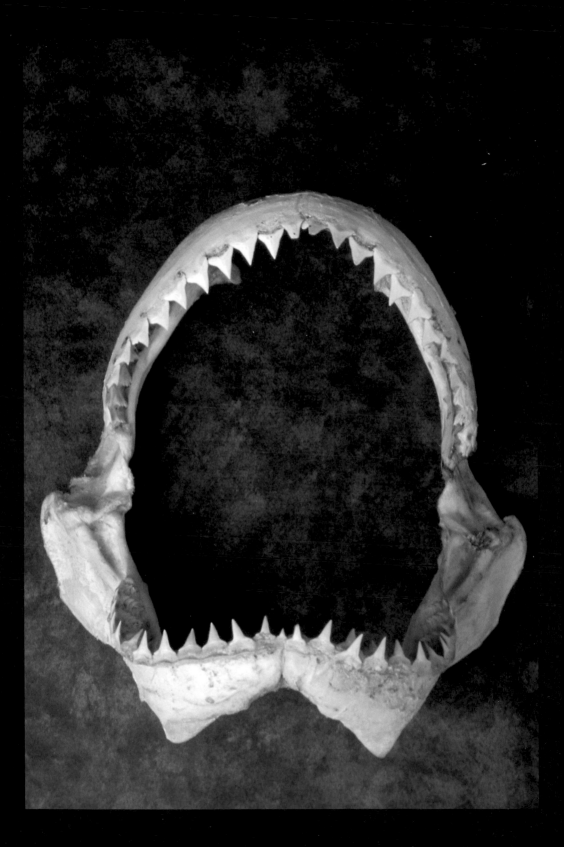

# Chapter One

# SHARKS: OUR FEARS AND FASCINATION

Centuries ago, a young boy named Kalani knelt in the stern of his father's fishing canoe, searching the cloudy sky for a single star. Early that morning, just before he and the crew had sailed away from Kaho'olawe (one of the islands that today makes up Hawaii), his father had given him the opportunity for which he'd longed most of his fourteen years. "Today, my son," his father said, "you will be leader." Finally, Kalani would have the chance to navigate the canoe. Today he would prove he was old enough to be a captain of his father's fishing crew.

The Kaho'olawe crew members were rough seafaring men, and Kalani's father was the most seasoned of them all. His coarse and calloused hands showed the world he was an

*Sharks belong to the Chondrichthyes class. There are between 350 and 400 different species whose ancestors can be traced back over 450 million years.*

Do you see this image as frightening? Or beautiful? How you think of sharks will depend a lot on the messages you've absorbed about these animals from the culture around you.

experienced fisherman, and the ocean's spray had ocean-matted his long, graying hair into thick, salty locks. Kalani knew his own hands were too soft, delicate, and his hair was light and thin, unstained by the sea's tempests. The crew members liked to call him baby names. But today, Kalani was determined to prove to them and to his father that he was a man.

However, now that he had finally had his opportunity, he felt as though the gods must be working against him. The fish had hidden from the crew, and now a storm rolled across the sky, pulling a blanket of thick clouds across the stars. Kalani needed those tiny lights to find his way home. He could see no land anywhere, not the tiniest line along the horizon, and he didn't want to ask the crewmen or his father for help. He had to prove himself on his own.

This medieval drawing portrays sharks and other ocean creatures as they were imagined during the Middle Ages: as sea monsters.

Ahead of him, in the bow of the small boat, Kalani's father faced away from the crew. As the canoe leaped and fell across the waves, Kalani saw the crewmen watching the back of his father's head; he saw their lips move, as they prayed to the gods for his father to turn around and end this terrible test. From his place in the stern, Kalani desperately searched the sky for guidance. He could not fail his father. . . .

In the 1500s, in Europe, sharks were also feared. This drawing shows a shark attack.

Thunder boomed like the sound of a god's voice, and at the same moment, Kalani heard a loud splash near the stern where he knelt. His eyes darted across the inky water, seeking the source—but he saw nothing, and his heart sank. Would his father stand by and allow his son to lead them all to their deaths?

Then Kalani heard another splash, closer this time. Out of the corner of his eye, he saw a huge gray fin break through the surface of the water. With his heart in his throat, Kalani saw an enormous face looking up at him from the water. A shark. Kalani knew the story of Kalahiki, the shark-god of Kahoolawe; he had heard the stories since he was a baby, and now he was certain he knew exactly what this shark wanted. . . .

With the other men still distracted by the heaving waves, Kalani reached down into the hull of the canoe and grabbed a container of the crewmen's awa, a fermented beverage that made drinkers feel sleepy and relaxed. Leaning forward over the stern, Kalani poured the awa into the shark's mouth.

The shark gulped and gulped again. When the last drop had fallen into his mouth, he grinned a huge, toothy smile at Kalani—and then he turned, showing Kalani the way back to the shore of Kaho'olawe.

Once the crewmen's feet were planted on the solid earth, they cheered Kalani. His father looked him in the eyes. "You have made me proud," he said. "Come. Let us go home and tell your mother."

But there was something Kalani had to do first. Making an excuse to his father, he lingered by the shore. Then, once he was alone, he poured out another container of awa into the green water—a thank-you gift for his

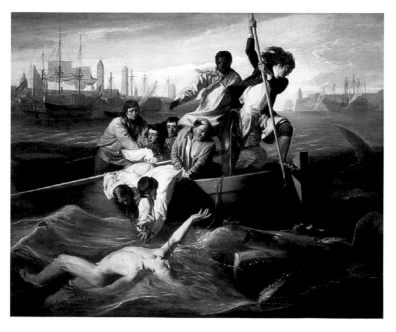

This painting depicts the rescue of Brooke Watson, a young orphan who was working on a trading vessel when the attack took place. The shark bit him before he was rescued, and his leg had to be amputated below the knee. It was rare to survive such traumatic episodes back in the eighteenth century, but Watson did survive. In fact, he grew up to serve as Lord Mayor of London!

# When Fear Is Fun

For those who do not harbor a serious phobic illness, the initial feeling of fear can develop into something pleasurable. Seeing, hearing, or reading about something we fear gets our blood flowing. Our brains receive a message that signals a reaction, so when we think about something we fear, we immediately feel a rush of sensations that begins in our brains and then races through our bodies. Our skin gets goosebumps all over, our knees shake, we scream out, or our hair stands on end. And sometimes, when it is over, we want more! We want to relive the whole smorgasbord of sensations. Fear and fascination made fisherman myths popular—the same way they now make newspapers with sensational headlines fly off the racks, and just as they make horror films blockbuster hits.

new friend, Kalahiki, the smiling shark-god who had brought them safely home.

## SHARKS' BAD REPUTATION

When the shark first appeared in the story, what did you think was going to happen? Did you think the shark was going jump out of the water and sink its rows of dagger-like teeth into the fishermen? Did it surprise you that this Hawaiian folktale personified the shark in a kindly way?

When those of us who live in North America today see the word "shark," we hear in our minds the ominous *Jaws* theme song, and our skins ripple with fear and aversion. We think of sharks as cold, heartless beasts that ferociously attack anything in sight. Most of us, however, have never—and will never—see a shark up close and personal in the wild. We don't really understand what makes a shark tick. The things we believe about sharks have been fed to us by movies and stories.

Meanwhile, sharks are a commonplace fact of life for the **indigenous** peoples of the Hawaiian Islands. After all, when you live on an island surrounded by water, you become familiar with the ocean and its creatures, including sharks. These people understand sharks. So it's interesting that native Hawaiians don't **demonize** these creatures of the deep; instead, most native Hawaiians respect sharks for their unrivaled beauty and power.

*Most shark species rely on constant movement in order to breath. Unlike most fish who have swim bladders, sharks rely on their oil-filled livers to stay afloat. If they stop moving, their own livers would cause them to sink.*

**indigenous:** refers to those plants and animals that are native to a particular region or country.

**demonize:** to portray as evil, like a demon.

## NATIVE ISLANDERS' PERSPECTIVE ON SHARKS

Like Kalani, most Hawaiians have grown up hearing the stories about shark gods that were passed down by their ancestors. One of the most popular sharks gods is Kalahiki (he also goes by the name of Kamohoali'i), who helps lost ships find their way in exchange for a narcotic **elixir** known as awa. Another common Hawaiian shark god is Moho, the revered protector of the seas, responsible for rescuing drowning people, guarding against intruders, and helping frustrated fishermen make a worthy catch. Many of the Hawaiian shark gods are protective spirits, while others are good-natured but mischievous tricksters. The creature known as Shark Man, for example, who could transform from shark to man and then back again, warned swimmers

**elixir:**
a sweetened mixture of alcohol, water, and medicine.

During colonial times, sharks were feared as dangerous sea monsters. This drawing shows a fishing ship's encounter with a shark. The shark lost this encounter!

# Get the Facts

The superage of information wields a double-edged sword. We have so many more avenues available to us from which we can gather information, but we cannot always be sure what we are seeing, hearing, and reading is true. In the end, you have a responsibility for your own education. Not every Web site is reputable; not every movie portrays the facts. It's okay to seek out entertainment, so long as you don't mistake it for truth. Do your homework. Sort the facts from the fables.

**afterlife:**
the life that
is believed
to exist after
death.

**shamans:**
the members
of a tribal
group who
act as priests,
or spiritual
guides, and
who use magic
to bridge the
gap between
the visible
world and the
invisible spirit
world.

**homage:**
a gift given
to pay tribute
to a higher
power.

The movie
*Jaws* entered
the world's
imagination in
1975, and has
been shaping
perceptions
of sharks ever
since.

of dangers. When he was in human form, he had a shark's mouth on his back, which he kept covered to conceal his identity. If swimmers did not heed his warning, however, Shark Man sometimes attacked them to teach them a lesson.

To other indigenous islanders, such as the inhabitants of the Solomon Islands in the southwest Pacific, sharks played a role in the **afterlife**. Powerful human beings often came back after death in sharks' bodies, which was considered a great honor. Some Solomon Island **shamans** even swam with sharks as part of their worship of the shark gods.

The myths and legends of numerous seafaring peoples, including those of Vietnam, Japan, the Fiji Islands, and parts of South America, also present sharks in a far different light from the modern North American attitude. The Vietnamese, for example, were once known for giving sacred burials to the bones of whale sharks. The ancient Japanese honored their own version of Shark Man, a god of storms known as Same-Hito. Some Fiji Island tribes gave **homage** to Dakuwaqa, a shark god from whom the tribe chieftains were thought to have descended.

## WHY WE HATE SHARKS

So how did North Americans come to fear the same creatures that some cultures hold in such high regard?

There's a short answer: gossip!

The great
white shark
(Carcharodon
carcharias),
infamous for
its starring role
in the movie
*Jaws*, can reach
lengths of up to
20 ft and weigh
up to 5,000 lbs.

As for the longer answer, historically, our first experiences with sharks came via word of mouth. Unlike indigenous island peoples, the average North American had little or no contact with the vast and mysterious seas. While island and seafaring people survived by fishing in the ocean, landlocked folk lived off the land. The white man's great shark myths began simply as stories told by sailors passing the time, fascinating fare for **landlubbers**. Like any cultural legend, details tend to be exaggerated with each new telling—and the scarier the story, the more interesting it is!

As newspapers became a part of North America's daily life, stories could reach an even greater audience. By 1916, when sharks killed swimmers on the New Jersey shore, most people still thought of sharks as "sea monsters." Newspapers across the country jumped on the story and tapped into the public's fear of the unknown. **Sensationalized** headlines swept across the landbound continent—and newspapers made a fortune.

As the years went by, the media continued to play an all-important role in the way we view sharks. For whatever reason, human beings are fascinated by their own fears. Often, the media depends on this fascination to sell itself or to get higher ratings. If we cannot explain something and we cannot control it, then we fear it. In popular culture, sharks represent the frightening—and thrilling—unknown. We love to hate sharks.

**landlubbers:** people who have little experience with boats and the ocean.

**sensationalized:** to have printed news with the goal of arousing a strong emotional reaction through gruesome or vivid details.

## THE LEGACY OF *JAWS*

When you hear the word "shark," what's the first image that pops into your mind? If you're like the majority of North Americans,

People tend to think of sharks as monsters, when really they are just misunderstood. We are entering their domain when we swim or surf in the ocean and we should respect that fact.

you probably picture the famous scene from *Jaws* when the monstrous great white shark first bursts from the water. When director Steven Spielberg finished filming his blockbuster movie in 1975, he probably didn't realize that Bruce, his mechanical monster, would become the representative of the shark world.

*Jaws* the movie was based on a novel of the same name written by Peter Benchley. Bench-

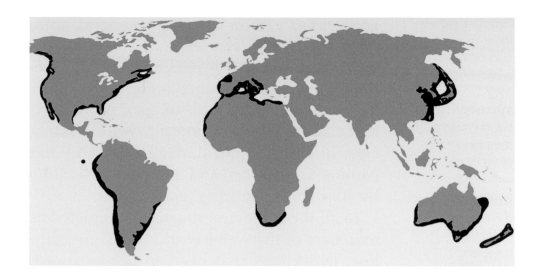

ley recalls, "I read about a fisherman who had caught a 4,550-pound great white shark off Long Island, and I thought to myself, 'What would happen if one of those came around and wouldn't go away?'" The novel that grew from this idea was published in 1974.

Clearly, Benchley's story tapped into the fertile soil of North Americans' fear. Benchley's shark was the overgrown child of all those long-ago seafarers' sea monsters. *Jaws* became an instant bestseller, selling over 20 million copies, and in the summer of 1975, Universal Studios released the movie. It grossed a record-breaking $100 million at the U.S. box office and $450 million worldwide.

Since its cinematic debut in 1975, *Jaws* has become a cultural phenomenon. Three sequels (by different directors and without the aid of Benchley) followed close on its heels, along with a *Jaws* theme-park ride and

The great white shark is found in temperate seas throughout much of the world. It is mainly found in the upper part of the water column in near shore waters. However, it can range from the surf line to far offshore and from the surface to depths of over 775 feet.

*Jaws* video games. Even the musical score from the movie (created by John Williams) has become instantly recognizable; it's **synonymous** with **imminent** danger. Other directors rode on the coattails of *Jaws'* popularity, and made their own shark movies, including *Deep Blue Sea* (1999), starring LL Cool J and Samuel L. Jackson, and more recently, *Into the Blue* (2005), starring Jessica Alba.

In all these movies, sharks are depicted as monsters of the water world. They are ruthless, evil killers that need to be destroyed. For most of us, these sensationalized and fictional stories make up the bulk of our information about sharks. Meanwhile, people who know sharks best (divers, researchers, and biologists) know the truth about these magnificent creatures.

**synonymous:** suggesting a relationship to; alike in meaning.

**imminent:** threatening; about to happen.

## RETHINKING *JAWS*

In the years after *Jaws*, attacks on sharks became more common. Many people believed sharks were deadly vermon that needed to be killed. The creatures seemed to have no redeeming virtues, and many people felt the seas should be rid of them.

Benchley was not prepared for what he called the "spasm of macho nonsense" that followed in the wake of his book, spurring people to hunt sharks and kill them. In 2002, twenty-eight years after the first publication of *Jaws*, Peter Benchley published *Shark Trouble*, where he apologized for the role he had

*Shark breeding habits are very brief, occur later in life, and don't involve lifelong mates. Some lay eggs, some keep eggs within their bodies, and some sharks give birth to live pups. The mother shark is not nurturing by nature and if the pups don't get away from their mother fast enough, they could become her next meal.*

played in demonizing sharks. In the decade before his death, he became a member of the National Council of Environmental Defense, championing the conservation of sharks and other sea creatures. On his Web site, Benchley stated, "I attributed to [sharks] a kind of marauding monsterism that became what *Jaws* was. Now we know that sharks do not attack boats."

So are sharks really kind, gently, cuddly creatures? Of course not. Like many wild animals, they can be dangerous to humans. They should always be treated

*A shark can live to be a hundred years old.*

with respect, and swimmers sharing sharks' waters should be aware of the safety measures they should take. Shark attack is a real danger that must be acknowledged by anyone who swims in the ocean—but it shouldn't be exaggerated.

*Megalodon (Carcharodon megalodon)* was a prehistoric shark that could grow to lengths of over 49 feet. Megalodon lived about 18 million to 1.5 million years ago and is thought to be an ancestor of the modern great white shark.

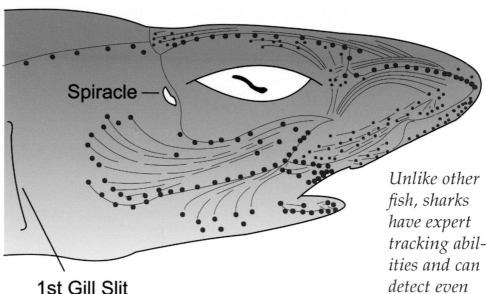

Spiracle

1st Gill Slit

*Unlike other fish, sharks have expert tracking abilities and can detect even the smallest electrical currents, tiny vibrations, and low-pitched sounds from as far as 100 yards away—all of which signal the location of potential prey. Sharks prefer to hunt alone, rather than in schools like other fish.*

To put things in perspective, consider these facts:

- Bees, wasps, and snakes are responsible for far more human deaths each year than are sharks.
- In the United States, the annual risk of death from lightning is 30 times greater than that from shark attack.
- The chances of dying while swimming in water where sharks live are much higher from many other causes (such as drowning and cardiac arrest) than from shark attack.
- Many more people are injured and killed on land while driving to and from the beach than by sharks in the water.

*Sharks and rays are a type of fish, but unlike most fish they are of the* Chondrichthyes *class, which means their bodies are made up of cartilage rather than bones. Because of this, sharks and rays cannot make quick stops or swim backwards, but they are more flexible and can turn around faster. Most rely on a weaving method to get around.*

- On any given day at the beach, you're far more likely to need a doctor's attention because of sunburn than because a shark attacked you.
- More people seek medical attention each year for jellyfish and stingray stings than for shark-related trauma.
- Many more sutures are used each year to sew the lacerations on peo-

ple's feet from stepping on sea shells than from shark bites.

- Out of approximately 400 shark species, only 11 have ever been reported as attacking a human (often by mistake), and only four are considered man-eaters.
- About 100 people are attacked by sharks each year. When you consider that the world population is well over 6,000,000,000, the chances that you will ever be attacked by a shark are pretty slim.

Like most wild animals, sharks do attack human beings. So let's see what we can learn from the people who have survived these attacks.

# Chapter Two

# EAST COAST FEAR: THE 1916 JERSEY SHORE ATTACKS

W hen Hermann Oelrichs dove headfirst into a sea of sharks in July of 1891, he was risking his life to put an end to an age-old fear—but mostly he was just showing off. By 1891, myths about monstrous sea creatures had faded. Sharks no later seemed quite so scary. In Hermann Oelrichs' mind, terrifying shark stories were merely old wives' tales. Earlier in 1891, he had published an article in the *New York Sun* offering a $500 reward for "such proof as a court would accept that in temperate waters one man, woman, or child, while alive, was ever attacked by a shark."

Oelrichs was a popular and successful shipping **mogul** who loved to entertain his famous friends (sometimes even Theodore Roosevelt) aboard his swanky yacht, the *Hildegard*. At six

**mogul:**
a businessman with a lot of money and power.

feet tall and over two hundred pounds, as powerful in stature as he was in business, he was well known for his boisterous arrogance. In July of 1891, while hosting a party on the *Hildegard*, he decided to accept his own challenge. When a group of sharks swam alongside the yacht, Oelrichs dove into the water and swam straight toward them.

His horrified guests watched as he kicked and splashed through the water. To everyone's amazement, the sharks fled. Amid the

One man, Hermann Oelrichs, had single-handedly changed the public perception of sharks by swimming unscathed with a school of them in 1891. In the summer of 1916, a lone shark would turn the tide against sharks once more.

applause of his guests, Oelrichs clambered triumphantly back onto the deck of his yacht.

Today, experts know the sharks were probably intimidated by the combination of massive yacht and large, flailing man. In Oelrichs' mind, however, and in the minds of his astounded guests, he had just single-handedly proven that human beings had nothing to fear from sharks. In reality, of course, Oelrichs was just awfully lucky!

In the fifteen years after Oelrichs' mighty swim with the fishes, not a single death from a shark attack was reported in North America. In 1906, Oelrichs died, smug in the knowledge that he had shattered an ancient myth. Most of North America was convinced, too. Scientists agreed that stories of man-eating sharks were mere legends. On August 2, 1915, *The New York Times* published an article asking the world to put the man-eating shark stories to rest for good. The article was entitled "Let Us Do Justice to Sharks," and it concluded that sharks could not be considered dangerous.

Just one year after the publication of this article, a different truth made its way to the shores of the United States.

*Four species of shark are considered to be dangerous: great whites, oceanic white tip sharks, bull sharks, and tiger sharks. Most people are most familiar with great whites, not because these sharks are the most aggressive, but because they spend part of the year swimming close to shore where many unsuspecting swimmers like to bathe.*

## FUN IN THE SUN

In 1916, the Jersey Shore had just entered an era of new popularity. The chug-chug of the Industrial Age was changing the world in

Beaches like the one at Asbury Park, NJ, were especially crowded in the summer of 1916 because of a heat wave and a polio epidemic. People were flocking to the Jersey Shore from Philadelphia and New York, and more people were actually venturing into the water than in the past.

many ways, including leisure time. The railroad tracks that now crossed the nation made transportation faster and easier; people were no longer tied as closely to their homes. They could travel now; they had access to places they had never been before—including the beach.

Once a pastime enjoyed only by the wealthy, beachgoing became a favorite recreation for Americans in the early twentieth century. It was a new era, one where even the lower classes now had leisure time, and beaches were within the reach of almost everyone who lived in the East. For people from New York and Philadelphia, the Jersey Shore was a favorite vacation destination. Meanwhile, the strict Victorian rules of conduct were fading into the past; at the beach, women showed more skin than they ever had before (although you could actually be arrested for showing too much skin); lovers met and romance flourished; cocktails, music, and good times abounded. In the summer of 1916, the only shadow across beach bathers' hearts was the worry that German **U-boats** might attack city seaports, including those along the Jersey Shore.

No one was worried about sharks.

## FOURTH OF JULY TERROR

The Engleside Hotel in Long Beach Island was one of New Jersey's most luxurious resorts, and in the summer of 1916, it was booked solid from Independence Day through Labor Day. Members of the wealthy Vansant family were among the 150 privileged guests vacationing there for the Fourth of July weekend.

On July 1, 1916, the Vansants took a stroll along the beach just before dinner. Their adult son, Charles, played with a dog by the waves. His family and a small group of other people watched the two dive into the ocean for a final swim before supper. As Charles swam further out to sea, the dog tried to keep up behind him—but suddenly, it turned and paddled to shore. Charles called for the dog

**U-boats:** German World War I and World War II military submarines; short for Unterseeboats, or undersea boats.

to come back and play, but the dog sensed something Charles couldn't: something had been out there in the water, swimming along-side them.

Shark attacks on the Jersey Shore, 1916

The 1916 New Jersey shark attacks began at Beach Haven, just north of Atlantic City. The shark moved northward, and the final attacks actually occurred in Matawan, NJ in the freshwater of Matawan Creek.

As Charles turned back to follow the dog toward land, someone on the beach noticed a fin following him. The crowd on the beach shouted, trying to warn him, but Charles couldn't hear their voices above the sound of the waves. When he was almost to shore, wading through just three and a half feet of water, rows of powerful teeth suddenly sank into his leg, just below the left knee.

A group of men ran into the water to rescue Charles, and the shark backed off, its ominous black fin sliding away through the water. A man named Alexander Ott reached Charles first and began to drag him to safety. Suddenly, Ott felt something pulling Charles in the opposite direction. The shark had come back for more.

This time it bit him in the thigh. According to Ott, the shark was roughly ten feet long and weighed about five hundred pounds. It took the strength of the entire group of men tugging against the immense power of the beast's jaws to finally free Charles. Witnesses claim that the shark was even pulled all the way onto shore, still attached to Charles's thigh, before it finally gave up and disappeared back into the ocean.

Charles Vansant was carried to the Engleside Hotel, where he bled to death within an hour. This was the first recorded case of a human attacked by a shark on American shores.

A week later, the news had reached other East Coast beach towns. No one was too worried, though. *The New York Times* slipped a small article into its pages titled "Dies After Attack by Fish"; otherwise, the attack received little press attention. In the early years of the twentieth century, the idea of a giant, human-hungry fish was the stuff of sailors' tales. Besides, no one wanted to damage the tourist business along the shore.

The fun in the sun was still going strong at the glamorous New Essex and Sussex Hotel in Spring Lake, even though it was only forty-five miles north from Beach Haven where Charles Vansant had died. People gossiped about the news, as people do, but the hotel staff and seasoned guests assured those who were new to the hotel that they'd never

Even in 1916 the media loved a good story, and the shark attacks created a media frenzy.

A great white with suspicious remains in its stomach was caught and declared to be the man-eater, and the attacks certainly ended with its demise. However, some scientists today debate that a bull shark (shown here) might have been a more likely culprit, because they more commonly swim into freshwater.

before heard of a shark attack on the Jersey Shore. Most folk chalked the story up to one of those sensational stories newspapers carry sometimes, giving it as much credit as you probably do when you see headlines at the grocery checkout claiming that aliens have landed.

## A NIGHTMARE COMES TO LIFE

Charles Bruder for one didn't worry about the story as he headed out to enjoy a swim during his work break on Thursday, July 6, 1916. Charles was the bell captain at the New Essex and Sussex Hotel, and he and the other members of his work crew enjoyed placing bets on who could swim out the furthest into the waves. On that July afternoon, the other bellhops were wary of the waves; they'd been hearing the gossip about the shark attack, and they didn't think they wanted to swim any races into the deeps for a while.

Meanwhile, Bruder insisted that there was no such thing as a man-eating shark and that the newspaper article was nothing more than a fantastic exaggeration. Bruder had worked at a hotel near Los Angeles the previous summer, and he claimed he had often swam alongside schools of leopard sharks that had never done him any harm. According to Bruder, Charles Vansant probably just drowned.

Eventually, the other men dove into the waves with Bruder, either because they had

*If a shark attack occurs in freshwater (like the Matawan Creek in New Jersey), bull sharks are the likely culprits; they are the only aggressive, man-eating, shark species that can survive in both salt water and freshwater.*

Great white sharks are known for their curiosity—they explore unfamiliar objects by biting them. Attacks on humans may result from this behavior, which can easily cause injury as a result of the shark's sharp teeth and the force of its jaws.

been convinced or because they didn't want to look like cowards. When Bruder swam under the safety ropes, however, his companions hung back, watching as Bruder kept swimming farther away from the shore. The water was only ten feet deep when he was attacked.

Guests along the shore later said they noticed a spot of red in the water; they thought Bruder was in a red canoe, waving for help. Lifeguards rowed quickly to him

# Common Survivor Reactions

According to psychologists, those who have survived a traumatic situation—whether it is an act of terrorism, a rape, a serious illness, or a shark attack—often experience similar emotions. The initial feelings are usually shock, pain, fear, and desperation. After a trauma, human beings tend to feel vulnerable. Their assumption that they are safe and immune to life's evils has been shattered. They have lost the control they thought they had over their lives. Individuals find many ways to cope with these feelings, some of them positive and some of them negative. Some survivors react by becoming extremely hostile and belligerent, diverting their pain and fear into a need for revenge.

*Sharks' skin is different from that of other fish. Most fish have smooth, round scales, but sharks have sharp scales shaped like tiny daggers known as denticles. Denticles make sharks very rough to the touch, and if a shark brushes past you, it can easily cause skin abrasions.*

and found a spreading pool of blood floating on the seawater. "A shark bit me!" Bruder called to them. He clung to the lifeguard's oar, and they hoisted him into their boat. His lightness amazed them.

To their horror, they soon realized why Bruder was so light: he had lost most of both legs. He was also missing a large chunk of flesh from his torso. They tried to wrap his wounds and staunch the flow of blood, but it pumped out too rapidly. As he faded into unconsciousness, Bruder said (according to the *New York Herald*'s report), "He's a big fellow and awful hungry." Bruder, like Vansant, died from blood loss.

A guest of the New Essex and Sussex Hotel was watching the scene from her window, and she called the hotel manager, David B. Plumer. Plumer was terrified and immediately sent out a coast-wide shark alarm, the first in U.S. history. Via switchboard, Plumer sent the shark warning to every hotel up and down the Jersey Shore. An experienced physician and fisherman named Dr. William G. Shauffler stated publicly, "There is not the slightest doubt that a man-eating shark inflicted the injuries." The next day the *New York Herald*'s headlines screamed, "Boy, Legs Bitten Off by Shark, Dies After Fight in the Surf." The *Philadelphia Public Ledger* cried, "Shark Kills Another Bather!" Thousands of beach-goers fled the shore and refused to return for the rest of the summer, some for the rest of their lives.

Sea-monster lore that had been dismissed as legend had suddenly leapt to life. A nightmare was swimming the seas in the light of day. The survivors of these shark attacks were terrified, and their terror was contagious. Panic swept along the East Coast. After panic, came the desire for revenge.

## FRESHWATER PANIC

Dr. Shauffler believed a single shark was responsible for both deaths, a **rogue** shark that needed to be terminated. Within hours of Bruder's death, Dr. Shauffler had already planned a massive sea patrol to hunt down and destroy the man-eating killer. The patrol

It is important to remember that sharks are not monsters, but vital members of the oceanic ecosystem. People must try to understand these creatures, even though sometimes they can be frightening.

**rogue:**
alone, dangerous and abnormal in behavior.

The great white shark is found all around the world because of its ability to regulate its body temperature. The great white is actually able to keep its body warmer than the water around it, allowing it to survive happily, even in cold water.

searched the seas for the beast, but they weren't prepared for where the next attack would hit.

The shark (or sharks) probably rounded Sandy Hook Peninsula to the north, where Charles Bruder had just been buried, and then entered Sandy Hook Bay. From there, it eventually swam into Matawan Creek, seventeen miles inland from its saltwater home. In this era decades before extensive shark research, few people knew that some shark species can live in fresh water.

In the afternoon of July 11, 1916, fourteen-year-old Rensselaer Cartan Jr. skipped out of work at the Lumber & Coal Company and went for a skinny-dip in the local swimming hole; his cousin, Johnson Cartan, and some other neighborhood boys went along. The water was dark and murky, but no one was worried about what might be lurking there. After all, their swimming hole was in a fresh-water creek.

Then Rensselaer felt something bump into his chest. He cried out, glimpsing a huge dark shape as something that felt like sandpaper scraped open his skin.

None of the other boys had seen anything. "Liar!" they laughed when he claimed to have just seen a shark. When Rensselaer went back to work, he told his tale again, but no one believed him; the townspeople assumed his story was the work of a young boy's imagination.

One person did believe him, however, an old sea captain. He kept his eyes open, and he too spotted a shark in the creek. But the captain was known for his tall tales, and no one believed him either.

A little while later, in the same town, young Lester Stilwell and his friends cut out of basket work for a dip in the creek, just as Rensselaer had done. Down on Dock Road, the boys dove and splashed. And then, as Lester Stilwell floated on his back, the other boys spotted a huge, dark shape swimming directly under him. Before they could react,

*Sharks have hinged jaws that can envelop large prey and swallow it whole. Most sharks possess 3 to 15 rows of teeth, while the whale shark has 310 rows of teeth! Some sharks have serrated teeth, and you can find shark tooth souvenirs all over the world because sharks often lose their teeth while eating. But don't worry—their teeth grow back the very next day!*

the shark reared up out of the water and sank its teeth into Lester's arm.

The other boys watched with horror as the shark shook Lester and then yanked him underwater. Lester burst above the water, flailing and screaming one last time. Then the shark pulled him under.

The boys raced toward town, screaming, "Shark!" Not many people believed them; most folk assumed that Lester must have hit his head or had some other mishap. Fearing he had drowned, they went down to the creek to look for poor young Lester Stilwell. When they could see nothing from a boat, two men, George Burlew and Stanley Fisher, dove into the dark water, searching the murky shadows for the unfortunate boy.

A half hour went by. Finally, the two men decided to make one last dive before they gave up. Burlew came up empty-handed and made his way to the dock, defeated. Then Fisher broke the water's surface, shouting that he had found the boy. Burlew dove back into the water to assist Fisher.

The water swooshed by his legs with such incredible force that Burlew stopped dead. Fisher, he realized, had not only found the young boy. He had also found Lester's killer.

Fisher cried out: now he was the one being attacked. As he kicked and punched the beast, the water turned red with his blood. Somehow, he managed to free himself from the shark's powerful jaws. Meanwhile, the other men hit the water with their hands and

A shark does lose teeth almost every time it eats, but some shark teeth that are for sale are obtained in an illegal fashion. An illegal market has arisen in the trade of great white teeth and jaws, because the numbers of these sharks are declining around the world.

oars to distract the shark while Fisher tried to make his way from the creek. He was almost there, still holding on to the body of young Lester Stilwell, when he screamed, let go of the body, and was pulled back into the water.

Matawan Creek is a tidal creek, meaning the water in the creek ebbs and flows with the daily tides. Because the mouth of the creek gets built up with sediment, a shark might swim upstream following food at high tide, and find itself stuck in the creek once the tide drops lower.

Amazingly, he fought off the shark a second time and made his way toward land. This time, however, Lester's body had disappeared. As Fisher dragged himself from the water, the crowd that had gathered saw he was missing most of the flesh on his right thigh.

Fisher maintained consciousness the entire time he waited for medical assistance. Help was too far away and came too slowly, however; Stanley Fisher bled to death, just as Vansant and Bruder had before him. Lester Stilwell's body was eventually found floating in the creek.

In modern times, news of ongoing events can spread around the world almost instantly, but in an age when newspapers and gossip were the most common means for spreading the word, news—even the most terrifying—traveled more slowly. The same day that Fisher and Lester had been attacked, three boys, Jerry Hollohan and Joseph and Michael Dunn who lived in Cliffwood, a mere three-quarters of a mile south, had no way of knowing what had just happened.

At four o'clock that afternoon, the boys were splashing in the middle of the creek when a man raced onto the dock, screaming, "Shark! Shark!" The boys swam as fast as they could back to the dock, but the warning had come too late. When Jerry Hollohan and Michael Dunn climbed onto the wooden planks, Joseph Dunn was still ten feet behind

When a great white shark gets ready to bite, its jaws extend forward as its head recedes back. The lower jaw strikes first, and then the upper jaw descends, until the upper and lower jaws fit together perfectly holding the prey tightly in place. This whole process takes less than one second.

them. Joseph felt something rough brush against his skin, and then teeth like daggers sank into his legs.

Meanwhile, two motorboats were making their way downstream, warning everyone they passed of the recent shark attacks. One of the men in the boats, Jacob Lefferts, saw what had happened to Joseph, and he immediately dove into the water. Joseph's brother Michael also rushed to his brother, and together, Lefferts and Michael managed to wrestle Joseph from the shark's massive jaws. They pulled him onto the dock, but his left leg dangled off the wood above the water—and the shark took one last bite before it finally retreated. Luckily, Joseph received medical care in time, and he survived the attack.

The shark must be stuck in the creek, people decided. Their enemy was confined. With wire nets to block its retreat and a $100 bounty to stir up the already surging lust for revenge, more than a hundred men patrolled the waters through the night, setting off dynamite and rifles at the smallest movement.

Spectators came from all over the Jersey Shore to watch the new sport: shark-hunting. A reporter from the *New York Times*, however, noticed that the wire fence the town had erected had been chewed through. The rogue shark had escaped.

## SHARK FRENZY

On the evening of July 14, 1916, a shark was spotted again. This time it butted a boat, but the fisherman escaped unharmed. Now, however, people believed they knew the shark's route. They were convinced it was headed for New York City.

The newspapers went wild with shark frenzy, warning bathers to beware. Some of the stories were very real. Others, however, were **fabricated** to feed the public's need for drama and excitement. Several shark encounters were reported to have happened on New York's Coney Island. Later, however, people admitted they might have just imagined these near misses with the beast.

**fabricated:** made-up; created; falsified.

Beach bathers had all fled the water. Instead, hunters swarmed the shore with spears and guns, waiting and hoping to be the heroic shark slayer. Dozens and dozens of sharks were killed in the hunt for the rogue man-eater. Sharks of all breeds were harpooned, dragged to shore, and then disemboweled in search of human remains. All anyone found were bellies full of fish.

A flurry of letters even reached the White House, begging President Woodrow Wilson to help find the rogue shark and make the waters safe again. Tourist resorts were suffering, and people were terrified. Wilson called on the U.S. Coast Guard to fight back. On July 15, 1916, the *Washington Post* ran a front-page headline titled "U.S. War on Sharks."

Days later, the mission to expel the Atlantic of all killer sharks was deemed impossible. The final decision was to either fence off swimming areas, or not allow any swimming at all. There was not much more you could do.

The last the public heard of the deadly rogue shark, a man named Michael Schleisser had allegedly caught it in a net four miles from the mouth of Matawan Creek. Schleisser bludgeoned the shark to death, dragged it to shore, and then cut it open. Inside the great white's body, he found human bones, which he then sent to the American Museum of Natural History for further confirmation. A **taxidermist** with a wall full of animal

**taxidermist:** the person whose job it is to prepare, stuff and mount the skins of animals.

heads already on display, Schleisser stuffed the beast and delivered it to the offices of the *Home News* newspaper to put on public display for two days. The headlines read, "Harlem Man in Tiny Boat Kills a 7 1/2 Foot Man-Eating Shark." People came in droves from all over to see it.

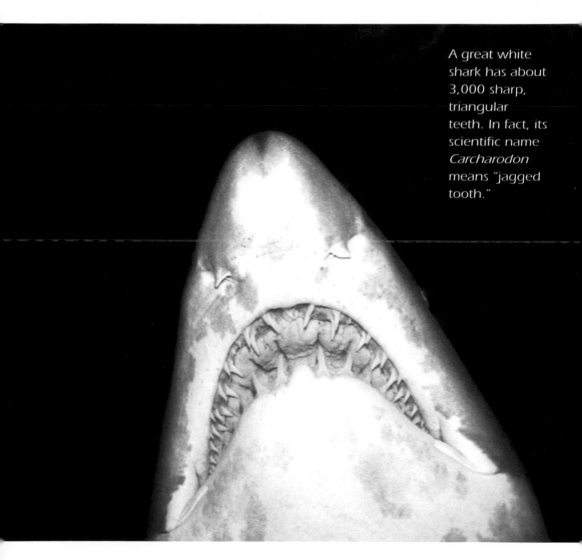

A great white shark has about 3,000 sharp, triangular teeth. In fact, its scientific name *Carcharodon* means "jagged tooth."

In the end, though, scientists could never determine whether the human bones found in Schleisser's shark were from the recent victims, or had come from already-dead remains the shark had scavenged. (Drownings along the Jersey Shore were not uncommon.) Specialists argued over the bones and how long they had been in the shark's stomach. Ultimately, no one could prove absolutely this was the sole shark responsible for all the 1916 Jersey Shore deaths. They couldn't even prove it was responsible for a single one.

Shortly after being put on display, the body of the great white shark disappeared and was never recovered. With its disappearance, the terrible summer of 1916 slowly faded from the public's consciousness, only to be resurrected in living color with the release of *Jaws* (said to be based in part on the Jersey Shore shark attacks).

## WHAT REALLY HAPPENED?

Today, scientists believe that it's unlikely that the string of attacks were the result of just one shark. What's more, great whites cannot survive in fresh water, but bull sharks can. Shark experts don't believe a single deranged shark obsessed with human flesh is a very likely scenario. Instead, so many people suddenly swimming in shark territory was more likely to have been the cause of all the attacks. Neither humans nor sharks were used to encountering each other.

## WHAT DOES IT MEAN TO SURVIVE A SHARK ATTACK?

If you had been a member of Charles Vansant's family, a coworker of Charles Bruder, or one of Lester Stilwell's friends, and had watched as a shark sank its teeth into your loved one or friend, how do you think you would feel about sharks? What if you had been Joseph Dunn, the only person to actually survive a shark's bite during the summer of 1916?

Of course, it would be only natural for you to fear and hate sharks. In your mind, sharks probably wouldn't merely equal danger; you'd also equate them with evil.

This normal human reaction is what triggered the blood lust for sharks after the Jersey Shore attacks. It's also what makes you want to slug the bully who beat up your little brother. And it's the same sort of reaction that gave rise to many of the emotions in Americans' hearts after the attack on Pearl Harbor (which led to U.S. involvement in the World War II) and the terrorist attacks of September 11, 2001 (which led eventually to the U.S. war in Iraq).

Dr. Ofer Zur, a psychologist who has spent much of his career studying the human response of hatred, believes that understanding based on accurate knowledge is the only way to transform this normal human response. He recommends something he calls "realistic empathy," which, he stresses, "does not mean that the enemy is not . . . hostile or dangerous, it only means that we recognize the . . . **catalysts** that motivate it to act." He goes on to say,

> If we can develop realistic **empathy**, many other *biases* will be reduced. We will be less likely to make hostile predictions, to have selective negative attention. . . . With this more realistic view of the enemy we are more likely to react and deal with situations more reasonably and thereby eliminate dangerous, paranoid, self-fulfilling prophesies. We will, hopefully, react to real threats in a realistic, appropriate and, above all, effective manner.

At the beginning of the twentieth-century, when the Jersey Shore shark attacks terrified the East Coast, most North Americans believed Nature and its inhabitants were there for human beings' convenience. And when Nature wasn't convenient—not to mention if it were downright dangerous to human life—it deserved to be destroyed. In fact, it needed to be destroyed. It only made sense.

As the U.S. government's campaign on sharks soon learned, however, it was impossible to truly eradicate all sharks from the deep. And if the Coast Guard could have accomplished its goal, what would the long-range effects on the Earth's interwoven

**catalysts:** things that spark great change or action.

**empathy:** the action of understanding the emotions of another without having actually gone through the same experiences.

ecology have been? Scientists today have learned to look at Nature as a whole—and sharks in particular—in a different way. Environmentalists tell us human life needs to learn to coexist successfully with other life on Earth—or all of us will suffer.

What many shark researchers **advocate** is a lot like Dr. Zur's realistic empathy. If we understand sharks—rather than turn them into horrifying monsters—we can learn to protect ourselves from their danger, while at the same time appreciating their reality.

On the ReefQuest Centre for Shark Research Web site, shark expert R. Aidan Martin, has this to say about sharks:

> Like any wild animal, sharks will defend themselves if threatened. Despite their reputation for ferocity, sharks are actually remarkably non-violent creatures. If a shark "feels" threatened—due to being pursued, grabbed, speared, or otherwise molested—it will most likely either swim away or attempt to signal its unease by way of a specific display, a kind of "body language." . . . Among the most obvious of these is a pronounced lowering of the pectoral fins, the paired, wing-like fins located behind the gill slits. If this warning is ignored, the shark may swim away rapidly or launch a lightning fast, slashing attack. Since we are the visitors in the sharks'

living room, the **onus** is on us to be a well-behaved guest, to recognize their signals, and to respond appropriately.

**onus:** burden; obligation.

However, during the first half of the twentieth century, such an enlightened attitude was still far from the minds of most North Americans. Unfortunately, as the century wore on, new attacks only swelled sharks' terrifying reputation.

# Chapter Three

# SCAVENGER SHARKS: SURVIVORS OF THE USS *INDIANAPOLIS*

S harks and wartime don't make a good mix. And neither do ignorance and sharks. If you find yourself dumped from the frying pan into the fire (or surviving a shipwreck only to be surrounded by hungry sharks), it's better to understand what you're facing. When it comes to swimming with sharks, most of us wouldn't be as lucky as tycoon Hermann Oelrichs was. And for many of the crew of the USS *Indianapolis*, wartime plus sharks plus ignorance was an equation that added up to death.

## A DANGEROUS MISSION

On July 16, 1945, after much needed repairs, the USS *Indianapolis* left the port of San Francisco for what would be its final, fatal, mission.

The USS *Indianapolis* at Pearl Harbor in 1937.

**radiologist:** a doctor specializing in the use of X-rays (radioactive material) in the diagnosis and treatment of disease.

The mission of the USS *Indianapolis* was so top secret that not even the ship's captain, Captain Charles Butler McVay III, knew what it was until they were already at sea. More than a thousand men (some of them not much more than boys) were called in from all over to board the *Indy*; rumor had it they were headed for Japan. Finally, McVay confirmed their fears: they were headed for the war zone.

After departing Mare Island Navy Yard, the *Indy* stopped at Hunters Point, another navy yard near San Francisco. There, armed marines covered the dock. Two army trucks arrived and unloaded a huge wooden crate and a black metal canister onto the *Indy*. Not even the captain was told what it was. The only two men on board who knew the contents of the mysterious cargo for sure were Captain James Nolan, a **radiologist**,

and Major Robert Furman, a weapons intelligence engineer.

The USS *Indianapolis* had been entrusted with a very important mission: transporting the components of an atomic bomb. In the black metal canister was half of all the uranium-235 in the United States' possession, worth approximately $300 million. It would eventually be made into an atomic bomb that the United States dropped on Hiroshima,

The *Indianapolis* delivered the uranium and other components of the atomic bomb known as "Little Boy," which was dropped on Hiroshima, Japan on August 6, 1945.

En route from Tinian Island to Guam, the *Indianapolis* was struck and sunk by Japanese submarine torpedoes. It only took minutes for the ship to sink, leaving the surviving crew members floating in the open ocean.

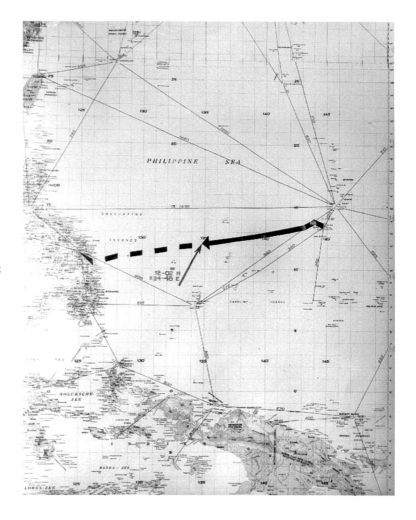

Japan, on August 6, 1945, killing more than 100,000 people.

On July 16, 1945, the USS *Indianapolis* charged ahead with its secret mission to deliver its very delicate cargo. The *Indy* left San Francisco unescorted by any other ships. She reached Tinian Island safely and in record time, where the cargo was unloaded. The next stop on the ship's route would be Guam. After that, the *Indianapolis* was scheduled to go to Leyte, where the ship would undergo drills before rejoining the Pacific Fleet for the planned invasion of Japan. Everything seemed to be going well. But then, things started going terribly wrong.

The *Indy* anchored in Guam safely. However, on the next leg of their trip to Leyte, the *Indianapolis* was denied escort destroyer ships because none were available. This made the ship vulnerable: the *Indy* did not have **sonar** gear, so it couldn't easily detect submarines. (Destroyers are specially constructed to defend ships like the *Indianapolis* against subs.) However, McVay was assured that they had nothing to fear. He was instructed to follow a zigzag pattern, which would make the ship harder for a submarine to hit; at night he could stop the zigzag at his own discretion.

**sonar:** equipment using the emitting and reflection of sound waves to detect the presence of objects (especially underwater); the word comes from the phrase SOund NAvigation Ranging.

## DEADLY MISCOMMUNICATION

What McVay wasn't told was that just three days earlier, a destroyer escort had been torpedoed en route to Leyte and 112 men were killed. He also wasn't informed that the Japanese group known as the Tamon was actively operating in submarines near the route the *Indy* was taking. Commodore James Carter neglected to inform McVay of all this because he assumed someone else would relay it in his routing orders. He was wrong.

On the *Indy*'s way to Guam, another message was sent out informing Rear Admiral

After the *Indianapolis* sank, the crew members who survived the initial torpedo impact, and managed to survive the leap into the water were only faced with further danger in the form of many different species of sharks tormenting them from all sides.

McCormick of the ship's expected arrival in Leyte. The message was received and transcribed correctly, but Admiral McCormick assumed the *Indy* would be shifted north to replace the USS *Portland*, a cruiser that was out of service. The second message, containing the expected date of the *Indy*'s arrival in Leyte, never reached its other party, Admiral Oldendorf. This miscommunication would prove fatal to many of the men aboard the USS *Indianapolis*.

On July 29, 1945, between 7:30 and 8:00 p.m., the *Indy* encountered rough waves, and Captain McVay ordered that the cruiser cease her zigzagging technique for the night. McVay went off to steal a few hours of sleep, telling the night watchman to notify him if he resumed zigzagging when the weather improved.

No one knew that lurking below the water's surface was I-58, a Japanese submarine commanded by Lieutenant Commander

Some of the sharks had probably been following the USS *Indianapolis* for days, attracted by the smell of waste thrown overboard. Modern military ships also encounter sharks while out at sea—here a shark attacks a U.S. Navy surveillance towed array sensor system (SURTASS) cable.

Hashimoto. The I-58 had picked up on sonar disturbances earlier that day, and by 11 p.m. that night, the sub captain spied a ship silhouetted by the moonlight: the USS *Indianapolis*, just six miles away. The *I-58* re-submerged and headed under water toward the *Indy*, undetected due to the *Indy*'s lack of sonar capabilities. At 11:09 p.m., Hashimoto ordered six torpedoes to be loaded and aimed directly at the unsuspecting *Indy*. At 12:04 a.m. on July 30, 1945, Hashimoto ordered, "Fire!" At 12:05 a.m., the *Indy* was hit.

According to survivors, only two torpedoes hit their target, but two were more than enough. Men were shocked from their slumber, gas tanks exploded, smokestacks spewed cinders, and everything, including the water below, was set ablaze. The bow of the *Indy* was completely missing, the cruiser ripped almost in half, and as the *Indy* continued to speed uncontrollably ahead, the ocean roared in to fill the void.

All communication systems were down, and in just a matter of minutes the entire cruiser would be down, too. Approximately a hundred men had already died on impact. Perhaps they were the lucky ones.

Eight minutes after the *Indy* was hit, Captain McVay had no choice but to shout, "Abandon ship!" Nearly 900 crewmen followed the order and leapt off the ship into the cold, dark water. Some rafts and lifejackets were distributed, but many men leapt overboard without anything. The ship had two emergency whaleboats (light boats used to transport crewmembers when the ship was in a harbor), but amid all the chaos, neither could be dislodged in time.

In a matter of minutes the *Indy* had shifted to a ninety-degree angle and was sinking. Some crewmen quickly wrote letters home; others kissed pictures of their girlfriends good-bye. One man ate a sandwich before jumping ship. Some, never forgetting their duties as military men, tried to dispose of classified documents they had been guarding. Many crewmen helped each other, while others decided it was every man for himself. One sailor stopped to clip his toenails just before jumping ship.

Before the *Indy* sank completely, the radio technician, Jack Miner, was able to use a light switch to send off an SOS with the ship's coordinates. In a radio shack in Leyte, Clair B. Young received the message. Young immediately brought the message to

The survivors of the *Indianapolis* were finally rescued in a massive operation that took six days. Many of the survivors were taken to Guam aboard the hospital ship USS *Tranquility*.

Commodore Jacob Jacobson, but Jacobson was not concerned. He told Young to notify him again only if a second message was received. A sailor at another location in Leyte also received the distress call, but his commanding officer, Commodore Gillette, was playing bridge when the distress call was received. Another officer on duty responded by sending two navy tugboats to the *Indy*'s rescue, but when Commodore Gillette learned that this decision had been made without his authority, he demanded that the tugboats return, even though they had already been traveling toward the location for seven hours. The last message was received at a landing craft docked in Leyte; Russell Hertz tried to radio an answer back to the *Indy*—but it had already sunk. Hertz rushed the message to the Leyte naval base, but again, it was ignored. According to Doug

## Shark Fact

The first step in sharks' eating habits is to circle and assess. Then they usually bump or nudge to figure out exactly what's in front of them. This minimal contact with sharks' sandpaper-like skin can actually cause bloody gashes. What the shark is doing is testing the object, deciding whether or not it is worth eating. Unlike the common assumption that sharks attack suddenly and without consideration, ruthless and vicious in their attempts to consume anything and everything, sharks actually put a lot of thought into their feeding.

**protocol:**
a set of rules
that must be
strictly followed.

Stanton, author of *In Harm's Way*, "the prevailing **protocol** within naval command was that messages that couldn't be confirmed by a reply were to be disregarded as pranks." But how were they supposed to receive a reply from a sunken ship?

As the man responsible for all the lives onboard the *Indianapolis*, McVay must have

## Shark Fact

If sharks decide to take a bite, they then decide whether the taste is to their liking. If it's a sea lion, which they love, they'll return for a second bite and attempt to devour the unlucky animal whole. If it's a human, they may leave it because they prefer fattier mammals, or they may settle for it if they're particularly hungry. If a shark is feeling weak or the prey is looking hefty, the shark will usually take one bite and then let the prey bleed to death before coming back for more; that way it doesn't have to use more energy than it needs to.

hesitated before abandoning the sinking warship, wondering whether to stay with his ship or take his chances in the water. In the end, Nature made the decision for him when a massive wave swept him off the deck and into the sea. As he floated in the oily water, Captain McVay comforted himself with the thought that the *Indy* was expected to arrive at Leyte in the next thirty-six hours. Surely, someone on Leyte would send help when the ship did not arrive on time. He did not know that the hour of their expected arrival had never been properly conveyed to Leyte.

## OUT OF THE FRYING PAN . . .

Nearly 900 men either dove off the ship or were swept into the water along with their captain. Much of the lifesaving gear had slid off the *Indy* on the **starboard** side. The 325 men who jumped from that side were either wise or lucky and grabbed the first flotation device that drifted past them. The men on the other side had no such luck or foresight. The black fuel oil leaked from the hull into the water, poisoning many of the men, who died almost immediately, overcome by the shock of the searing fluid that filled their bodies. Meanwhile, the cooks, laundresses, and most of the doctors were trapped in the lower compartments of the ship.

The men who had escaped the ship on the starboard side collected five floater nets, four rafts, and some food and water. Led by Dr.

**starboard:** the right side of a ship; opposite of port.

# Shark Facts

The great white (*Carcharodon carcharias*) is the biggest and most powerful shark with the worst reputation. These sharks use a "bump and bite" technique—they bite their prey and let it bleed to death before devouring it—but they prefer to eat sea lions, rather than humans. Great whites have 3,000 serrated teeth; their teeth are the largest of all shark species. They've even been known to attack boats, crushing the hull with their snouts. They are on average 18 to 25 feet long and weigh between 4,000 and 7,000 pounds. They swim in deep waters part of the year, and then close to shore for the rest of the year. Their main hangouts? Australia, New York, Massachusetts, and California.

Haynes and Father Conway, the nets were arranged to hold the 200 wounded men who could not swim, with one net reserved as a place for those who were not injured to occasionally rest. With few paddles and no compasses, they had little hope of reaching land on their own. Many men prayed aloud and tried to boost each other's morale, reassuring their comrades and themselves that help would surely be sent when the *Indy* did not arrive in Leyte on time.

Captain McVay eventually drifted across the path of one of the rafts and was pulled to safety, where he assumed leadership of the group. Meanwhile, another group of nearly 300 drifted on their own as well, haphazardly led by Ensign Harlan Twible and Richard Redmayne. Twible demanded that the men all remove their shoes because they were weighing them down. When Jack Miner leaned over to take off his shoes, he caught his first glimpse of something swimming right below him.

## . . . AND INTO THE FIRE

As the men drifted further from the oil spill, the sun rose and the water cleared. The survivors of the initial danger now began to worry about a new peril: sea creatures bit and clung to their limbs.

At first, when the crew felt something bumping against their legs in the water, they

*Kicking or punching a shark in the snout is a good defense method; hitting it in the eyes is even more effective.*

*Sharks prefer to feed in low light. They have their breakfast just before dawn breaks, and they eat their dinner at dusk, before night falls.*

Oceanic white tips (*Carcharhinus longimanus*) are relatively common in the deep waters of the tropics. They are normally solitary sharks, but may join with other white tips in a feeding frenzy when a large food source is present.

assumed they were feeling the limbs of their fellow crewmen. Exhausted, hot (during the day, the temperatures near the Equator were above 100° Fahrenheit (38° Celsius), the men would drift off into sleep, only to be jolted awake by another bump. Were they imagining it? They were in close contact with hundreds of other men—but something told them no human had touched them. They wondered if they were starting to lose their minds.

Planes flew overheard, but no one saw them. McVay, in an effort to maintain his

# Shark Facts

The bull shark (*Carcharhinus leucas*) is not as well known as the great white, but it's potentially the most dangerous. These sharks like to travel and are the most adaptive shark, thriving in salt water, brackish water, and freshwater. They are stout looking, but smaller than the great white, growing to between 7 and 11 feet and weighing 200 to 500 pounds. They prefer water that is waist-deep to about ninety feet in depth, especially rivers, preferring to feed in brackish water at river mouths during the summer. They are less picky than great whites about what they eat and will gladly eat humans. When many great whites were killed for sport along the East Coast, bull sharks had no larger shark species to keep them in check, and their populations increased. Bull sharks are the actual culprits for many deaths previously blamed on great whites. Although they can attack swimmers, for some reason they tend to avoid divers. Their favorite hangouts? Papua New Guinea and Australia.

# What Makes a Survivor?

According to Laurence Gonzales, author of *Deep Survival*, successful survivors go through the same patterns of thought and behavior as they keep themselves alive. Gonzales says, "It doesn't seem to matter whether they are surviving being lost in the wilderness or battling cancer, whether they're struggling through divorce or facing a business catastrophe—the strategies remain the same." Here are Gonzales' twelve Rules of Survival:

1. Perceive and believe. (Don't deny the reality of your situation.)
2. Stay calm, but use your anger to keep you motivated.
3. Think, analyze, and plan.
4. Take correct and decisive action.
5. Celebrate even your smallest successes.
6. Be a rescuer, not a victim. (Help others who share your dilemma.)
7. Enjoy the survival journey. (Sing, play games, tell jokes, recite poetry.)
8. See the world's beauty. (This may seem silly—who's going to be looking at the beautiful sunset with sharks nudging against their legs? But, explains Gonzales, "The appreciation of beauty, the feeling of awe, opens the senses to the environment. [When you see something beautiful, your pupils actually dilate.]"

Gonzales tells the story of Debbie Kiley and four others who were adrift in the Atlantic after their boat sank in a hurricane in 1982. "They had no supplies, no water, and would die without rescue. Two of the crewmembers drank seawater and went mad. When one of them jumped overboard and was being eaten by sharks directly under their dinghy, Kiley felt as if she, too, were going mad, and told herself, 'Focus on the sky, on the beauty there.'" Kiley survived.)

9. Believe you will succeed.

10. Surrender. (This seems just the opposite from Rule #9—but Gonzales explains, "Yes you might die. In fact, you will die—we all do. But perhaps it doesn't have to be today. Don't let it worry you. Forget about rescue. Everything you need is inside you already. Dougal Robertson, a sailor who was cast away at sea for thirty-eight days after his boat sank, advised thinking of survival this way: 'Rescue will come as a welcome interruption of . . . the survival voyage.'")

11. Do whatever is necessary. (Some survivors have even drunk their own urine!)

12. Never give up.

Gonzales concludes: "A survival experience is an incomparable gift: It will tell you who you really are."

# Shark Facts

The tiger shark (*Galeocerdo cuvieri*) is thought to be the second deadliest to humans (after the bull shark). The tiger shark doesn't travel as much as the bull shark, however. Tiger sharks' teeth are serrated and curved in a hook-liked shape. Their heads and mouths are broader than other sharks, and they are striped; they average 11 to 14 feet in length and weigh up to 2,000 pounds. Tiger sharks will eat anything (a headless man in complete armor was once found in the stomach of a tiger shark), but like bull sharks, they avoid divers. They prefer shallow water in tropical climates. Their favorite hangouts? South Africa, Australia, the Philippines, the Caribbean, and especially Hawaii.

own sanity, continued official business, logging each passing plane in a notebook. He tried to keep his crew positive by suggesting they do the same, assigning rescue lookout times to each of them in turn, to keep their minds focused on survival. By the time the sun had set on their first full day adrift, however, morale had plummeted.

All the while, deep in the dark sea, sharks were keeping company with the luckless crew of the USS *Indianapolis*. The creatures had probably been following the ship for days, eating refuse thrown off its deck. If any sharks in the area hadn't already been paying attention, they would have been thoroughly roused by the vibrations as the ship exploded and sank. Now, however, something far more interesting had captured their attention: the scent of blood leaking into the water. As night settled in around the drifting *Indy* crewmen, the sharks were still assessing the situation. By dawn the following morning, they had made their decision.

The survivors of the USS *Indianapolis* remember the daylight revealing an assortment of sharks around them: tiger sharks, makos, blue sharks, and white-tips. Gus Kay, a first-class seaman, recalled,

They stalked for hours, going around and around. And somebody said, "Those are PT boats!" And another guy said, "No, those are sharks! It's the wake

Hundreds of sharks circled the crew of the USS *Indianapolis*, while they waited and waited for help that took too long to come.

they make!" Finally, they attacked—pulled guys right out of the water. We thrashed, trying to keep 'em away from us, but they came right into the group. Took the net and everything right up into the air. Tore guys' limbs off. The water was bloody.

# Shark Facts

Oceanic white tips (*Carcharhinus longimanus*) sometimes travel in schools—and when they get together, they can be a nasty bunch. They prefer to remain in very deep waters in the tropics and are usually responsible for scavenging on the hapless victims of plane crashes and shipwrecks. (These sharks were probably the most active participants in the attacks on the survivors of the USS *Indianapolis*). Like tiger sharks, white tips will eat almost anything, including the dead. They like to follow schools of prey, especially dolphins, and they have been known to attack divers swimming with dolphins. The tips of their fins are white, and they average about 10 feet in length, weighing in at roughly 300 pounds. They rarely give a signal before they attack, and they are not shy about approaching potential prey as soon as they spot it. These are perhaps the most unpredictable of all sharks, making them very dangerous.

Captain McVay faced his own horror. One by one, his men disappeared around him, without a trace, or a sound.

The sharks had probably started with the dead bodies first. Next, they preyed on the men who had drifted away from the group. And once the vulnerable and the dead were devoured, the sharks moved on to live prey. The men with the least amount of clothing were the first to be eaten. (Sharks are often attracted to the way light reflects off pale skin.)

The Navy did not tell its men about sharks during World War II; the official position was that such information would only cause unnecessary fear. The drifting men flailed their arms and legs and thrashed about to scare off the sharks. They should have done exactly the opposite and remained perfectly still.

One by one, the sharks fed on the floating men. Some men were pulled straight under water, while others were simply eaten up to the waist and left as floating torsos. Some men fought back against the sharks, punching and kicking them in the snouts or plunging whatever sharp objects they had into the shark's thick skin. The sharks continued to circle, and the death toll rose.

McVay and his group quickly learned that sharks are intelligent problem solvers. When one shark found a hole in a raft, he shoved his snout through it and snapped, enlarging

# What Is Survivor Guilt?

According to psychologist Dr. Donna Marzo, survivor guilt is often experienced by those who escape from a disaster that seriously injures and kills others. Individuals dealing with this particular type of guilt may believe they experienced good fortune at others' expense, that by saving their own lives, they let others down. They may feel helpless, powerless, sad, and full of shame. Their sense of self and competence has been violently shattered by the traumatic events they experienced. Survivor guilt can stick with a person for years after the event that triggered it, making it impossible for the individual to pick up his or her life and go on. Those who are truly survivors must find a way to transform this normal reaction, often by helping others in difficult circumstances or by pouring their feelings into some sort of creative activity, such as art or writing.

**WARNING**

**Sharks may be present**

**Shark bites have occured in this area**

Signs like this remind swimmers and surfers that sharks might be sharing the water with them.

the hole in order to get to the humans on board. After his initial shock, McVay kicked the shark in the eye with his bare foot—and it retreated.

Meanwhile, Dr. Haynes watched as hundreds of sharks circled his group. Most were ten feet long. The pattern of attacks became the rhythm of the long, terrifying days: the sharks would attack in the morning, then cruise through the wounded and the dying all day, feeding again at night on the living.

The groups slowly drifted further apart. By the end of the second day, most of the surviving crewmen were bloodied by the sharks, and swollen and raw from contact with the salty water. Sharks weren't their only enemies out there in the ocean. The more the men bled, the more they attracted other kinds of **opportunistic** sea life as well. Barracudas and other fish bit their flesh and wounds.

Hypothermia was another enemy the men faced. Although the water was relatively warm, it was about twenty degrees colder than the human body's natural core temperature of 98.6° F (37° C). The *Indy* crewmen experienced a slow and steady decline in their body temperatures as the days dragged on.

**opportunistic:** taking advantage of a situation; feeding on whatever food is available.

## A TRAGEDY OF ERRORS

The USS *Indianapolis*'s proposed arrival date at Leyte came and went. Some navy personnel marked that the cruiser had reached port

# What Is Post-Traumatic Stress Disorder?

Post-traumatic stress disorder (PTSD) is a psychological disorder that causes individuals to emotionally re-experience scary and stressful events. Symptoms of PTSD can be terrifying, since while they are occurring, the person may be unable to tell the difference between memories and current reality. Memories that seem like they're happening all over again may disrupt a person's life and make daily activities difficult. These symptoms usually start soon after the traumatic event, but they may not happen until months or years later. They also may come and go over many years.

without checking. Others noted that the ship was late, but no one investigated why. Hundreds of ships came and went every day, and the USS *Indianapolis* simply got lost in the shuffle. Just a two-hour plane trip away, the surviving crewmen continued to drift and disappear.

After floating in the open sea for forty hours, only about 600 of the 1,196 crewmen originally aboard the USS *Indianapolis* were still alive. Some 200 men had died in the last twenty-four hours alone. After this point, many men gave up and chose suicide; they calmly removed their life vests and surrendered themselves to the sea. Overcome with thirst, some crewmen drank the seawater, a deadly decision.

Many of the men were soon hallucinating and delirious. One man cried out that a Japanese soldier was next to him; the others punched and kicked at each other to fight off the invisible enemy. Men drowned each other and gouged out each other's eyes. In ten minutes, what had started as one man's hallucination lead to the deaths of fifty men. By the third day, about one man died every ten minutes.

On the fourth day, Thursday, August 2, 1945, while patrolling the waters in a PV-1 bomber plane, Lieutenant Chuck Gwinn noticed an oil spill and lowered his plane to search for a Japanese vessel. Ready to drop bombs on an enemy, instead he spotted four groups of men. He immediately sent for help.

Up until the last minute, men continued to die. Some, still hallucinating, refused to be rescued; they thought their Japanese enemy was attacking them again. Sharks attacked others even while they were on their way to their rescuer.

The rescue of the survivors of the torpedoed USS *Indianapolis*, carried out by eleven aircrafts and eleven ships, is considered one of the largest sea rescues in U.S. history. It took six days to recover as many bodies as they could. The total casualties were astronomical: of the 1,196 crewmembers who had sailed from Guam, only 321 had survived. In less than a week, four more would die in military hospitals, reducing the total number of survivors to 317. Of the nearly 900 men who died, about 200 were victims of shark attack. The sharks had killed on average fifty men a day.

It's not always easy to be a survivor. As Captain McVay discovered, survivor guilt is a very real reaction to traumatic events like those experienced by the crew of the USS *Indianapolis*. To add insult to injury, he was **court-martialed** for "failing to zigzag": the military courts blamed him for the USS *Indianapolis*'s demise because he made the judgment call to temporarily stop zigzagging during a stormy night, even though he was told he could. The captain already felt responsible for the loss of so many lives, and as the years went on, his guilt eventually consumed him. In the end, he was the last

**court-martialed:** a military trial by a special court consisting of commissioned officers of the armed forces.

casualty of those terrible events in 1945: Captain Charles Butler McVay III took his own life on November 6, 1968.

Other *Indy* survivors, however, celebrated their gift of life. Years later, they continue to have reunions in Indianapolis, Indiana, where they reflect on the harrowing experience they shared. Through the years, they have offered each other support, becoming lifelong friends and brothers. Many of them were tormented with nightmares. **Post-traumatic stress** plagued some. But they built their lives anew, as all survivors must do in the wake of tragedy.

By now, the United States had received a rousing wake-up call to the danger of sharks. Never again did such large-scale attacks take place as had happened on the Jersey Shore in 1916 and in the tropical waters of 1945. But people continued to swim in the ocean, and shark attacks continue to occur.

**Post-traumatic stress:** a psychological reaction to a terrifying event, which can cause depression anxiety, flashbacks, and impaired social function.

# Chapter Four

# SURFER SHARK ATTACKS: BETHANY HAMILTON

S urvivors of shark attacks, like survivors of most anything, deal with their experiences in different ways. Until you actually live through the experience, it's impossible to say how you'd do in similar circumstances. One thing is clear, though: people who manage to find something positive in even the most horrible events are the ones who are able to rise above their experience. They're not victims; they're truly survivors.

## BETHANY'S STORY

You'd be hard-pressed to find a more positive person than world-renowned surfer Bethany Hamilton.

Before Bethany's birth, her parents moved to Hawaii for the beauty and the temperate climate—but mainly for the surfing. They were both avid surfers, and they instilled their life-long desire to catch the perfect wave in their daughter. Born in North Shore, Kauai, on February 8, 1990, Bethany learned to surf just a couple of years after she learned how to walk.

The four-year-old girl seemed to have an innate aptitude for the sport, and she was soon competing in contests all around the Hawaiian Islands. While in grade school, she garnered first place in "push and ride" in a surfing contest founded by the internationally renowned Quicksilver company. Next, she competed in her first major competition, the Rell Sun contest. Competing within her own age group, eight-year-old Bethany won first place in competitions involving two kinds of surf boards, the long board and the short board. The next year, she won the 1999 Haleiwa Menehune Championships. At the Volcom Puffer Fish contest, she showed her "girl power" and won second place in the boys' twelve-and-under category.

By the time Bethany was thirteen years old, the surfing community was already proud of her. The Rip Curl surfing gear company sponsored her, giving her the financial support she needed to pursue a life-long career in professional surfing. If she were already this good, what would she achieve in the years ahead? Bethany's life was a dream come true.

Then came Halloween day, October 31, 2003. Bethany was lying on her beloved

Hawaii is a surfer's paradise, and people come from all over the world to catch the monster waves along the North Shore of Kauai.

board after surfing since early that morning along Kauai's North Shore with three of her friends, Holt, Alana, and Byron Blanchard. As she relaxed in the water's gentle rocking, her left arm dangled in the ocean below her. Perhaps she was dreaming of her future—but her peaceful daydreams were shattered in an instant. A tiger shark snapped at her arm as it hung in the ocean.

Two years after the incident, Bethany described the shark attack to CNN:

> My left arm was laying in the water and my other arm was just holding on to my board and the shark just, like came up and attacked me and it, kind of pulled me back and forth. It was about a two- to three-second period and when it . . . was attacking me all I saw was like a gray blur.

The 10- to 15-foot long shark tore off Bethany's arm just below the shoulder. Then it disappeared, taking her arm with it.

Bethany's friends swam to her as fast as they could and helped her to shore. Her friend's father made a **tourniquet** out of a leash from one of their surfboards and tied it around the top of Bethany's arm. Then he rushed her to Wilcox Memorial Hospital, where her father was coincidentally undergoing knee surgery that morning.

The wound was about 16 inches long and 8 inches wide. The makeshift tourniquet kept

**tourniquet:** a band wrapped around a wound to slow, or stop, blood flow by constricting blood vessels.

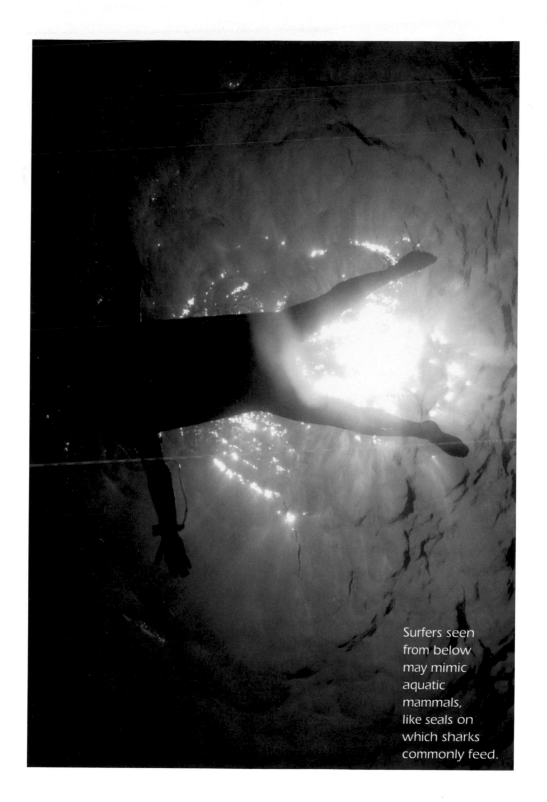

Surfers seen from below may mimic aquatic mammals, like seals on which sharks commonly feed.

The tiger shark (*Galeocerdo cuvier*) is common around islands in the pacific. It gets its name from the dark stripes that line the body of young sharks— the stripes fade as the shark ages.

Bethany from bleeding to death and saved her life. Bethany prayed all the way to the hospital, but by the time the ambulance arrived, she had already lost 70 percent of her blood.

At first, no one thought Bethany would live. Bethany proved everyone wrong. Once her condition became stable, the next question on everyone's minds was, "Will she ever surf again?" It didn't seem likely.

But Bethany had no doubts. She credits her faith in God with getting her through her experience. That, coupled with the fact Bethany was in great physical condition, contributed to an incredibly speedy recovery. But Bethany had lost all her left arm except her

# Faith and Survival

Research has found that people with strong religious faith are more apt to successfully recover from traumatic events. Prayer and the belief that a higher spirit is watching over them aid many people in their recovery.

shoulder. Competitive surfing seemed out of the question.

## BACK ON HER BOARD

The Hawaiian Islands are surrounded by beautiful blue-green water and about 40 different species of sharks.

Bethany may have leapt her psychological hurdles with relative ease, but she also had physical challenges to overcome before she could get back on a board. With only one arm, paddling was suddenly much more dif-

ficult. She had expected that, but more confusing was the way her weight distribution had changed due to the missing arm. Bethany only need three tries, though—and then she was able to ride the wave all the way to shore. Tears of joy filled her eyes.

To the joy and disbelief of many, Bethany was back on her board just ten weeks after the shark attack. Bethany refused to let the loss of a limb get in the way of her aspirations. She could have sworn off swimming forever—no one would have blamed Bethany if she were too afraid to go back in the water. She could have harbored anger and hatred toward sharks. Everyone would have understood.

But Bethany refused to let a stroke of bad luck keep her away from the thing she loves most: riding her surfboard. She understands the ocean is an unpredictable place; she knows there are other sharks out there. But Bethany prays and sings through her fears. A year after the attack, she told CNN:

> I'm [surfing] to have fun and not be scared because it is pretty rare for someone to get attacked twice. . . . The day I got back on my board . . . it was not necessarily hard. I was just so glad to get back in the water, because I'd been anxious for like a week.

Bethany and her family also rely on simple common-sense tactics for avoiding future

Some scientists hypothesize that sharks do not like the taste of people because humans are not fatty enough. After the initial taste-test, a shark will let go, allowing a person to escape alive, though not unscarred.

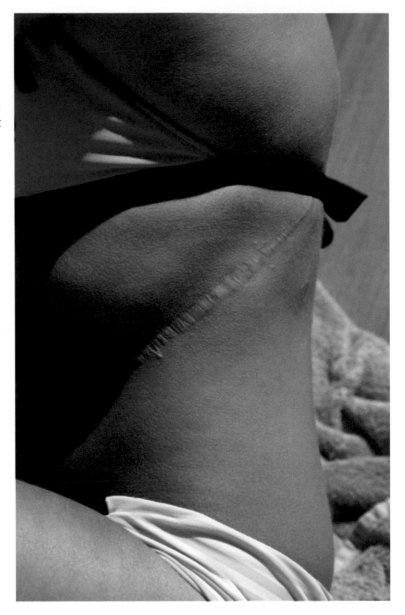

shark attacks. Bethany's mother, Cheri Hamilton, told ABC News that she and her family avoid surfing "at the worst hours of the day, during the sharks' feeding time—early morning or late at night."

Because they live in Hawaii, where the seas are heavily populated with sharks, the Hamiltons know they cannot avoid confrontation with the creatures altogether. Bethany has encountered several sharks since her attack; when she does, she gets herself to shore as soon as possible! She also uses a zebra-striped surfboard, which is thought to resemble a poisonous fish that sharks generally avoid.

Just getting back on a surfboard was accomplishment enough. But the same year she lost her arm, Bethany achieved what many had assumed was impossible: she placed fifth in the National Surfing Championships and garnered a position on the U.S. National Surfing Team. Later that year she was awarded the ESPY Award for Best Comeback Athlete of the Year as well as a Courage Award at the 2004 Teen Choice Awards.

Bethany didn't stop at surfing. If anything, her close call seemed to inspire her; she seized life with her single hand and refused to let go. No dream was impossible: after all, she'd overcome a shark! She faced life with renewed courage, determination, and hope.

In addition to sharing her courageous story with countless television programs, newspapers, and magazines, Bethany has also written a book about her experience. In 2004, MTV published her autobiography, *Soul Surfer: A True Story of Faith, Family, and Fighting to Get Back on the Board*; the book was

Bethany is not only surfing again, but winning again! Somehow this incredible young woman also finds time to design accessories, release albums, write books and inspire others through motivational speaking.

featured on the *Los Angeles Times* bestseller list. In 2005, just two years after the shark attack, Bethany achieved first place in the Explorer Women's division of the National Scholastic Surfing Association Nationals Championships. The same year, she released her own perfume and accessory lines. In 2007, a documentary film called *Heart of a Soul Surfer*, directed by Becky Baumgartner, featured Bethany's story. The following year, Bethany's first music album was released.

## Shark Facts

You can decrease the likelihood of being attacked by a shark by being especially careful in heavily shark-populated waters. Here are some quick stats about the hot spots.

### Unprovoked shark attacks recorded between 1670-2006:

United States: 944 unprovoked attacks; 55 fatal
   Hot spots: Florida, Hawaii, and California

Australia: 329 unprovoked attacks; 136 fatal
   Hot spots: New South Wales and Queensland

Africa: 276 unprovoked attacks; 70 fatal
   Hot spot: South Africa

You can check for updated information at the International Shark Attack Web site, www.flmnh.ufl.edu/fish/sharks/isaf/isaf.htm.

Bethany is also writing a young adult fiction series and several advice books for girls. She's a busy young woman, and clearly, having only one arm doesn't slow her down!

While Bethany continues to surf competitively, she also uses her experience to reach other people who face adversity. She takes being a role model very seriously, and this is the part of her life of which she is most proud. When she isn't surfing, she travels

Lesser predators, like these cow rays, flourish when the number of large sharks decreases. A small shift like this in a single ecosystem's balance can have much larger effects and long-term consequences for the health of the planet.

the world as a motivational speaker, lending her support to anyone who needs her. In April 2005, for example, Bethany visited U.S. troops in Germany who were being treated for injuries they'd suffered fighting in Iraq.

Every day, Bethany embraces the change in her body; she does not allow it to disable her. In fact, she barely uses her **prosthetic** arm. If she ever feels down about what happened to her, she always reminds herself of how much she has been able to achieve after the attack, deciding that, in fact, "more positive has come out of it than negative."

Bethany says, "[People] can do whatever they want if they just set their heart to it, and just never give up, and just go out there and do it." She is living proof that life goes on. She demonstrates what it truly means to be a survivor. In fact, Bethany Hamilton is not only a survivor, but a *thriver!*

**prosthetic:** relating to an artificial body part used to replace a missing or injured portion of the body.

# Chapter Five

# LESSENING THE ODDS: HOW TO AVOID ATTACKS

W̲e fear the things we don't understand.

Sharks have eluded our understanding and therefore plagued our nightmares. Even today scientists are only recently learning of the important place sharks hold in the ocean as apex, or top predators. As the top predators, sharks play a vital role in stabilizing the balance of the species beneath them in the food chain. If top predators disappear, the species beneath them (smaller sharks, skates and rays) increase in numbers. As a result, the numbers of smaller fish and shellfish that these lower carnivores eat decrease dramatically. Shellfish are important for filtering water, so when they disappear, water quality decreases. Poor water quality will in turn affect aquatic plant life along with many other animal species on which humans rely.

*Increased demand for shark cartilage is another threat sharks face. Some people believe that shark cartilage helps prevent and treat cancer, so health food stores carry shark cartilage. Unfortunately, the spines of about 100 sharks are needed to treat a single cancer patient for one year.*

Unfortunately, many species of sharks are decreasing because of overfishing by commercial and recreational fishing industries. Most of the sharks that are important to these industries are the largest predatory species. In addition, illegal shark finning and trade in shark teeth and cartilage lead to additional strain on shark populations. This decline could have dramatic effects on ocean ecosystems and human economies world wide. Education about the true nature and importance of sharks and an increase in conservation efforts will be important to prevent further population decline.

Truth is, sharks aren't evil. They're not ruthless killers with a taste for human flesh. They are wild animals, and like many wild animals, they have the potential to be dangerous—even deadly—to human beings. But from their perspective, it's nothing personal. They're simply doing whatever their natural instincts tell them.

Swimming in shark territory will always put you at risk. So if you're going to venture into a shark's domain, you need to follow some basic safety precautions. Mary L. Peachin, who has twenty years of experience diving with sharks, offers these guidelines in *The Complete Idiot's Guide to Sharks*:

1. Don't swim in the dark. As the crew of the USS *Indianapolis* learned, sharks like low lights and are prone to feed during the hours with the

least sunlight—so avoid swimming in water where sharks may live during the night, just before sunrise, or just after sunset.

2. Don't wear jewelry. Sharks appear to be attracted to jewelry, perhaps because they mistake it for the glint of a fish when the sun reflects off of it.

3. Don't swim with wounds. If you have an open wound that is bleeding, stay out of the water altogether. If you cut yourself while swimming,

Sharks often feed near river mouths or sandbars, so avoid swimming in these places. In this case, a great white shark following a food source swam into an estuary in Massachusetts.

*Sharks are a vital link in the sea's **ecosystems**. They are scavengers that help keep the water free of garbage and disease. By nature, they feed on the weak, which helps keep the gene pool strong. They also prevent overpopulation of certain species, maintaining the balance that Nature needs to thrive.*

**ecosystems:** communities of living things and their environments interacting and functioning as ecological units.

get out and stay out. Sharks are hypersensitive to the scent of blood.

4. Don't swim alone. Sharks prefer to attack solitary swimmers (whether humans or sea lions), because they're more vulnerable to attack—so stay with a group.

5. Don't swim near other animals that sharks consider food. This includes seals, sea lions, dolphins, and even dogs.

6. Don't swim near bait. Avoid swimming near fisherman and fishing vessels. Do not participate in diving expeditions that involve baiting, either. Feeding frenzies can prove fatal even to spectators.

7. Don't splash. Sharks can mistake splashing for indication of wounded prey. Try your best to swim like the fishes do: smoothly.

8. Don't go far from shore. Although certain shark breeds have been known to attack in just a few feet of water, it is best to swim within close range of help.

9. Don't swim near river mouths. Try not to swim in or near sandbars (often found at the mouths of rivers) or "steep drop-offs." These are both places where sharks like to look for food.

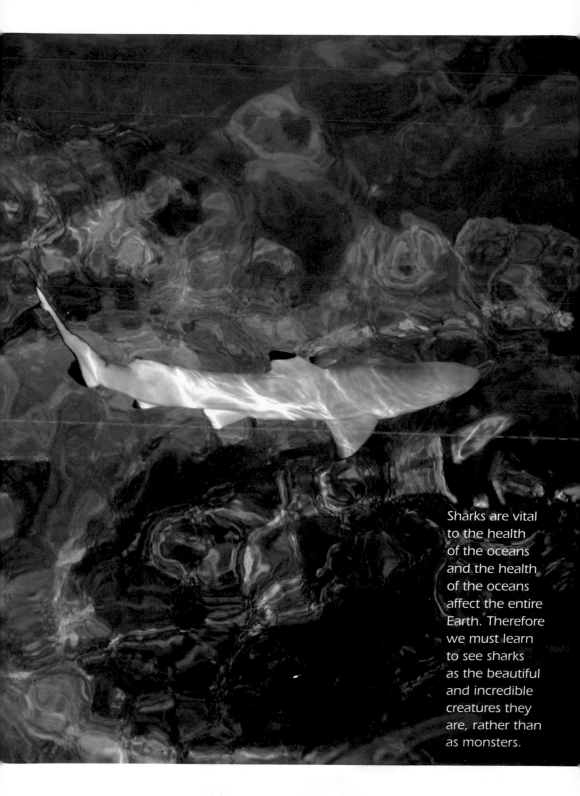

Sharks are vital to the health of the oceans and the health of the oceans affect the entire Earth. Therefore we must learn to see sharks as the beautiful and incredible creatures they are, rather than as monsters.

10. Don't ask to get attacked. Surprisingly, year after year, people are attacked—and sometimes killed—when they treat sharks like dolphins. They pull, grab, pet, or sometimes even try to ride the creatures, almost always with disastrous results. Sometimes a little bit of fear is a good thing. It shouldn't keep you out of the water entirely, but it

## Shark Facts

Sharks killings have increased over the past fifty years by 400 percent. Today, about 800,000 metric tons of sharks are taken from the ocean per year. That's more than 100 million sharks. Shark populations cannot survive this onslaught because, unlike many other fish, most large sharks don't reach sexual maturity until they are seven years old or even later, and then only give birth to a few pups each year. Shark researchers believe that twenty species of shark could become extinct by 2017, due—ultimately—to human greed.

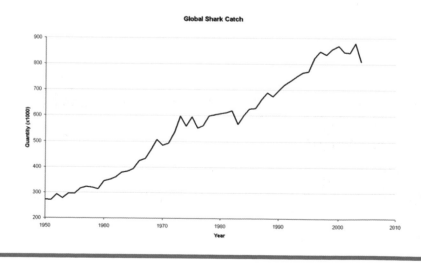

Global Shark Catch

# Shark Facts

Shark fins have become nearly worth their weight in gold. A single dorsal fin of a whale shark recently went for $15,000. Most fisherman don't have boats large enough to transport a large number of sharks, so many turn to finning, which doesn't require that they transport entire shark carcasses. (Finning means a shark is caught on a line, where it is often left for hours. When it is finally pulled on deck, its fins are cut off, and then it is thrown back into the water to die. Shark finning was banned in U.S. waters in December 2000 but it is still legal in other parts of the world.

should keep you at a safe distance from a potentially dangerous creature.

If you can remember this list of ten simple rules, you have already decreased your chances of getting attacked by a shark. Once you understand that your bracelet can attract sharks, that your splashing can draw sharks closer to you, or that you're more apt to encounter sharks at certain times of day, these creatures will no longer seem like such a mystery. Knowledge of basic first-aid techniques is also vitally important any time you're

*This sight near swimmers in the water can inspire fear and chaos, but learning some simple guidelines about sharks can help keep you safe while in their territory.*

**DANGER IN THE DEEP:** SURVIVING SHARK ATTACKS

swimming where a shark may bump into you. Remember, a tourniquet saved Bethany Hamilton's life.

What's the Golden Rule for dealing with sharks? Respect them. In a 1990s lecture at the Smithsonian Institution, *Jaws* author Peter Benchley said, "If I were to try to write *Jaws* today, I couldn't do it. Or, at least, the book I would write would be vastly different and, I surmise, much less successful. I see the sea today from a new perspective, not as an **antagonist** but as an ally, rife less with menace than with mystery and wonder. . . . And I know I am not alone. Scientists, swimmers, scuba divers, snorkelers, and sailors all are learning that the sea is worthy more of respect and protection than of fear and **exploitation**."

> ### Shark Facts
>
> - Each year falling coconuts kill more people in the world than sharks do.
> - Sharks may not like the way people taste. According to biologist George Burgess, in many shark attacks, humans receive only a single bite and then are spit out.

**antagonist:** an opponent or adversary.

**exploitation:** the act of using someone or something meanly or unfairly; taking advantage of someone or something.

Being a survivor means you know as much as you can about your situation; you separate your fears from reality. When it comes to sharks, this means learning about sharks, destroying the terrifying myths with the bright light of knowledge.

Be a survivor. Learn everything you can about what you fear (whether it's sharks or spiders, gang violence or AIDS, public speaking or diving off the high board). The danger may not go away—but you'll be in a better, stronger place to face it.

# Further Reading

Allen, Thomas. *The Shark Almanac*. Guilford, Conn.: Lyons Press, 2003.

————. *Shark Attacks*. Guilford, Conn.: Lyons Press, 2003.

Compagno, Leonard, Marc Dando, and Sarah Fowler. *Sharks of the World*. New York, N.Y.: Princeton, 2005.

Hamilton, Bethany. *Soul Surfer: A True Story of Faith, Family, and Fighting to Get Back on the Board*. New York, N.Y.: Pocket Books/MTV Books, 2004.

Parker, Steve, and Jane Parker. *The Encyclopedia of Sharks*. 2nd ed. Buffalo, N.Y.: Firefly Books, 2002.

Peachin, Mary L. *The Complete Idiot's Guide® to Sharks*. Indianapolis, Ind.: Alpha Books, 2003.

Stanton, Doug. *In Harm's Way: The Sinking of the USS and the Extraordinary Story of its Survivors*. Rockland, Mass.: Wheeler, 2001.

# For More Information

Bite-Back: Shark and Marine Conservation
www.bite-back.com/sharks.htm
The conservation-focused site for the United Kingdom's Bite-Back organization, which is dedicated to the protection of sharks. Visitors can learn more about the issues surrounding consumer demand for shark meat and fins and the group's campaigns to halt the senseless slaying of sharks.

The International Shark Attack File
www.flmnh.ufl.edu/fish/Sharks/ISAF/ISAF.
  htm
A site that includes information on more than 4,000 shark attacks, from the mid-1500s to present. The site is administered by the American Elasmobranch Society, an international group that studies sharks, skates and rays, and the Florida Museum of Natural History.

Monterey Bay Aquarium: Sharks: Myth & Mystery
www.mbayaq.org/efc/sharks.asp
Interactive and informative, this Web site offers visitors the opportunity to learn more about saving sharks and the dangers of modern fishing practices.

Peter Benchley
www.peterbenchley.com
Brief but informative site about Peter Benchley, the author of *Jaws*. Includes the rationale for writing the book and discusses Benchley's feelings about the image of sharks that *Jaws* produced, as well as his changed sentiment in the last decades of his life.

Shark Research Institute
www.sharks.org
The official Web site for the Shark Research Institute, a multi-disciplinary, non-profit scientific research organization that sponsors and conducts research on sharks and promotes the conservation of sharks. In addition to offering membership to the organization, the site boasts numerous educational and informative areas (many geared towards kids), including how to "adopt a shark."

Sharkwater
www.sharkwater.com/index.php
Supportive Web site for the documentary movie *Sharkwater*, which was released in late 2007. The movie was made by an award-winning filmmaker who joined up with a noted conservationist to uncover the exploitation and corruption surrounding the slaughtering of the world's shark populations in numerous marine reserves. The site includes supporting resources to the film, including a blog and study guides for students.

Publisher's note:
The Web sites listed on these pages were active at the time of publication. The publisher is not responsible for Web sites that have changed their addresses or discontinued operation since the date of publication. The publisher will review and update the Web-site list upon each reprint.

Allen, Thomas B. *Shark Attack: Their Causes and Avoidance*. New York, N.Y.: The Lyons Press, 2001.

Benchley, Peter. Peter Benchley's Website, www.peterbenchley.com.

Capuzzo, Michael. *Close to Shore: The Terrifying Shark Attacks of 1916*. New York, N.Y.: Random House, Inc, 2003.

CNN. "Then & Now: Bethany Hamilton." www.cnn.com/2005/US/05/09/cnn25.tan. hamilton.

Gonzales, Laurence. *Deep Survival*. New York, N.Y.: Norton, 2004.

Hamilton, Bethany. The Bethany Hamilton Web site, www.bethanyhamilton.com.

Hamilton, Bethany. *Soul Surfer: A True Story of Faith, Family, and Fighting to Get Back on the Board*. New York, N.Y.: Pocket Books/MTV Books, 2004.

Martin, R. Aidan. ReefQuest Centre for Shark Research Web site. www.reefquest.com.

Parker, Steve, and Jane Parker. *The Encyclopedia of Sharks*. 2nd ed. Buffalo, N.Y.: Firefly Books, 2002.

# Bibliography

Peachin, Mary L. *The Complete Idiot's Guide®*
*to Sharks*. Indianapolis, Ind.: Alpha Books,
2003.

Stanton, Doug. I*n Harm's Way: The Sinking*
*of the USS* Indianapolis *and the Extraordi-*
*nary Story of its Survivors*. Rockland, Mass.:
Wheeler, 2001.

Zur, Ofer. "The Love of Hating: The Psy-
chology of Hating." www.zurinstitute.com/
enmity.html.

# Index

# Index

# Picture Credits

NOAA
  Skomal, Greg: p. 114
  Theberge, Captain Albert E.: p. 38

Universal Pictures: p. 19

United States Department of the Interior
  Watt, James: p. 66–67

United States Navy: p. 68
  Maksinchuk, Steven: p. 113

To the best knowledge of the publisher, all images not specifically credited are in the public domain. If any image has been inadvertently uncredited, please notify Harding House Publishing Service, 220 Front Street, Vestal, New York 13850, so that credit can be given in future printings.

# About the Author and the Consultant

## Author

Joyce Zoldak lives in New York City and works for the nonprofit sector. She will be pursuing a Master's degree in Urban Policy in Fall 2009.

## Consultant

Andrew M. Kleiman, M.D. is a Clinical Instructor in Psychiatry at New York University School of Medicine. He received a BA in philosophy from the University of Michigan, and graduated from Tulane University School of Medicine. Dr. Kleiman completed his internship, residency, and fellowship in psychiatry at New York University and Bellevue Hospital. He is currently in private practice in Manhattan and teaches at New York University School of Medicine.